RICHARD BUNDUKI
Pathy MAKOYI

Modern-day ethics

RICHARD BUNDUKI
Pathy MAKOYI

Modern-day ethics

Ethical considerations in research: a multidimensional approach

ScienciaScripts

Imprint

Cover image: www.ingimage.com

This book is a translation from the original published under ISBN 978-620-6-72812-2.

Publisher:
Sciencia Scripts
is a trademark of
Dodo Books Indian Ocean Ltd. and OmniScriptum S.R.L publishing group

120 High Road, East Finchley, London, N2 9ED, United Kingdom
Str. Armeneasca 28/1, office 1, Chisinau MD-2012, Republic of Moldova, Europe
Managing Directors: Ieva Konstantinova, Victoria Ursu
info@omniscriptum.com

Printed at: see last page
ISBN: 978-620-8-50978-1

Summary

This book explores critical aspects of research ethics and methodology in several distinct studies. The overall theme is the pursuit of rigorous, reliable and ethically sound research practices, particularly in the social sciences and public health. The articles systematically highlight the complexities and challenges involved in achieving these goals, advocating nuanced approaches that consider both theoretical frameworks and practical applications.

The first part looks at identifying research gaps and implications for future research. It examines the differences between French- and English-speaking approaches to research, highlighting the limits of exclusive reliance on qualitative or quantitative methods. The authors highlight the impact of socio-economic factors, including funding and access to resources, on research outcomes. They stress the need to go beyond a simplistic dichotomy and adopt mixed-method approaches to enhance the validity and reliability of research. The influence of evolving technologies, such as AI and the Internet, is discussed both as a potential solution to existing shortcomings and as a source of new ethical considerations.

The second part focuses on the benefits and challenges of using triangulation in research. The authors provide a detailed analysis of its applications in qualitative, quantitative and mixed methods approaches. They highlight the benefits of triangulation in improving the validity, credibility and robustness of research results, while acknowledging methodological obstacles and resource considerations. The section highlights the complexity of integrating multiple data sources and methods, but points to the overall increase in robustness of results when done correctly.

The third part focuses on the ethical considerations involved in maintaining the confidentiality, integrity and rights of participants in scientific research. It traces the historical context of research ethics, emphasizing the need for informed consent, protection of participants and prevention of bias. This section examines the ethical implications of new technologies, such as AI, for data collection and analysis, reinforcing the importance of up-to-date guidelines and protocols. The authors raise awareness of the potential for technological advances to create new ethical dilemmas, requiring a proactive and vigilant approach to responsible research practices.

The fourth part analyzes remuneration policies in the public health sector in the DRC and their impact on service quality. It examines the gaps between policy and practice, identifying a significant gap between intended policy objectives and actual outcomes. Using a mixed-methods approach, the research highlights the crucial need for fair and transparent remuneration to ensure the well-being of healthcare professionals and improve service quality. The study highlights the complex interplay between economic, political and societal factors influencing the issue.

In summary, this collection of research papers makes a significant contribution to the understanding and advancement of responsible research practices. It underscores the need for a multi-dimensional approach that takes into account methodological rigor, ethical considerations and socio-economic realities. The diverse research topics and methods explored in this compilation reinforce the importance of a critical and self-reflexive approach to research, arguing for continued vigilance in efforts to improve the ethical and methodological standards of research in various disciplines.

Introduction

This compilation of research articles explores the multifaceted landscape of ethical and methodological considerations in contemporary research practices, with a particular focus on the social sciences and public health sectors. The overarching theme that unites these diverse studies is the pursuit of rigorous, reliable and ethically grounded research that makes a significant contribution to knowledge while upholding the highest standards of integrity and accountability. The articles presented here collectively address the critical challenges and complexities faced by researchers in achieving these ambitious goals.

The inherent tension between the quest for knowledge and the ethical imperative to protect human subjects is a recurring motif in these studies. While the advancement of knowledge remains a central objective, the ethical considerations surrounding research methodologies and their implications for participants are constantly brought to the fore. This importance reflects a growing awareness of the potential for biases, both conscious and unconscious, to influence research results, and of the profound impact that research can have on individuals and communities. The articles explore the delicate balance researchers must strike between rigorous inquiry and safeguarding human dignity and well-being.

What's more, the studies collectively illustrate the limits of simplistic approaches to research. The inadequacy of relying solely on qualitative or quantitative methods is highlighted, arguing for a more nuanced and sophisticated approach, such as mixed-method research strategies and triangulation. This emphasis on methodological pluralism recognizes the complexity of social phenomena and the need to adopt multiple perspectives to ensure robust and reliable results. The articles demonstrate that a comprehensive understanding often requires the integration of diverse data sources and analysis techniques.

In addition, the research presented here takes an active interest in the changing technological landscape and its implications for research practices. The increasing availability and use of powerful technologies, including artificial intelligence and big data, necessitates a reassessment of established ethical guidelines and the development of new protocols to ensure responsible data collection, analysis and interpretation. The ethical dimensions of AI in research are addressed, warning of potential biases and the need for transparency and accountability in the use of these powerful tools.

Finally, the inclusion of a case study on remuneration policies in the public health sector in the DRC highlights the practical implications of ethical and methodological considerations. The research highlights the significant impact of socio-economic factors on research results, and the need to address these disparities in the design of research projects. The survey emphasizes the imperative of ensuring equity and justice in research practices, demonstrating how the theoretical frameworks discussed throughout the compilation translate into tangible, concrete consequences. This collection is thus a valuable resource for researchers, policy-makers and anyone concerned with the ethical and methodological conduct of research.

In essence, this collection of studies offers a rich and multifaceted exploration of the crucial issues facing contemporary research. It underscores the need for ongoing dialogue and critical reflection on the ethical and methodological challenges researchers face in navigating the increasingly complex landscape of research and technology. It calls for a commitment to rigorous, ethical and socially responsible research practices that benefit both humanity and the advancement of knowledge.

Identifying research gaps for future research

future research

1. Introduction

From the point of view of general observation, any structure, mechanism or management system has a rhythm of operation, and this is relative to each sector.

Starting from existential facts (past) and through our observation, we can identify strengths that are independent variables (X) in the present and have a positive influence on the expected pattern (Y), which represents weaknesses to be improved. As Grawitz Madeleine points out in her book Méthodes des sciences sociales, *"The task is not to contemplate what no one has yet contemplated, but to meditate as no one has yet meditated on what everyone has before their eyes"*. (Grawitz, M., 1993)

And following this detection, establish a diagnosis (theory) focusing on one or more shortcomings requiring either readjustment or updating to bring more effective performance.

To achieve this objective, we need to examine the shortcomings that have been identified, and above all propose reliable and valid methods (innovations) that can be supported, with a view to remedying them for better performance.

As supported in the theory of authors Müller-Bloch & Kranz, stipulating that: "*Every research project must, in one way or another, address a gap, i.e. attempt to fill a piece of information missing from the Literature. Otherwise, it is not new research and therefore does not contribute to the general aims of science.*" (Müller-Bloch & Kranz, 2015).

In order to contribute to the general objectives of science, we will analyze the approaches of two linguistic giants, France and the United States of America, to standards of scientific communication and publication.

2. Francophone approach

It should be noted that this standard has revolutionized scientific research by granting researchers scholarships and giving them access to industrial research training agreements. This has opened up the field to the socio-economic category. In addition to its benefits, this standard of scientific research is described as being more focused on "*qualitative*" research, because it is long-term in nature, requiring more time to collect, analyze and process primary data before establishing validity and reliability, and before publishing results deemed irrefutable in accordance with pre-established standards (Müller-Bloch & Kranz, 2015).

3. Anglophone approach.

In addition, American research standards make it easier for researchers to access libraries and databases. This is in stark contrast to the French approach, which is based on long-term fieldwork that is not compatible with American requirements.

As English has become a world language, its adoption as such should not influence the principles of research. However, as a communication tool, it should favour the propensity of other research that conforms to standards, whatever their language of publication. Furthermore, the socio-economic aspect of the English-language approach should not be the keystone and sine qua non for data to be considered reliable and valid. (Michel, B., 2004).

This being the case, in order to identify and trace the implications of future research, we will draw out the gaps identified and established in the research carried out using these two approaches.

4. Gaps in research.

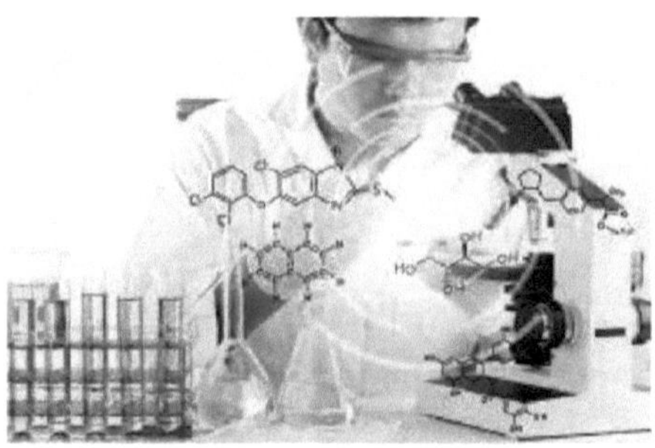

Starting from the outline of further readings we found that there was a convincing gap in both the English and French approaches and this in a systematic way on the 7 aspects of the gaps which are: *"Evidence gap Knowledge gap, Practical knowledge gap, Methodological gap, Empirical gap, Theoretical gap, Population gap"* (Müller-Bloch & Kranz, 2014).

We note that conclusions made and widely accepted in the past were contradicted by new research results, but several centuries later.

But now, with the advent of the internet and artificial intelligence (AI) and their use in scientific research and management, these kinds of gaps can be filled in a short space of time by automating repetitive tasks, freeing up researchers' time to concentrate on higher-level cognitive activities.

5. Research implications for the future.

As any researcher, we can't talk about the future without questioning history, and it's worth remembering that research is subject to particular contexts, including the influences of time (the era) and environment (***level of understanding, beliefs and convictions, social and community norms***), depending on whether research is seen as a means of improving society or not. But also, is research a subject of interest to practitioners? Is critical thinking accepted or not? It's by tackling this aspect of things that we can better inform our research for the future.

For ages, many scientists have been either valued by their society or rejected by it. In **1642, Galileo *Galilei*** met his death for supporting an existing Copernican thesis, in which he developed a theory asserting that the earth rotates on itself and around the sun.

We can therefore note that research is also influenced by the "***political, media, socio-economic and cultural***" environment, hence a society where critical thinking was not accepted in that era, and the researcher was condemned to death (Ferrand, F., 2018).

Examples are legion, and we can also point to a number of other shortcomings in the development of the Covid-19 vaccine. It's worth pointing out that distrust of vaccination is not new or unchanging: as far back as the 19th century in France, the creation of the Louis Pasteur Institute sparked off a strong protest following its research experiments, notably on : - animal experimentation. For some researchers, this is one of the precursory signs heralding current refutations of "Big Pharma" (Crié, D., 2022).

Indeed, after a comparative study of the research standards derived from the Anglophone and Francophone approaches, our analysis of the implications of future research must take into account the following aspects: a confrontation of the research conclusions derived from the "*qualitative*" approach resulting from primary data with those of secondary studies based on the "*quantitative*" approach referring to libraries and data banks, in the interest of considerably reducing the gaps and refutations after the research. This confrontation will take the form of literature synthesis, consultation of respondents, consultation of audiences, request for information addressed to researchers, and finally an evaluation and contextual analysis report.

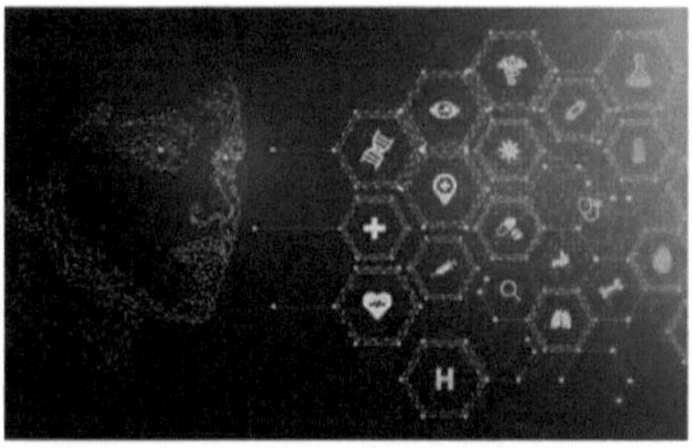

We can't talk about the implications of research without mentioning the use of the Internet and artificial intelligence (AI) in scientific research.

The use of these tools has revolutionized the field of research, making it easier for researchers to manage large quantities of data, extract relevant information and carry out repetitive tasks automatically.

As a result, the adoption of these powerful tools by researchers should be done by maintaining a balance between human ingenuity and the automation generated by Artificial Intelligence, while keeping in mind the limits that these tools may have, but also the implications for research ethics, namely: "*Data bias and fairness, Privacy and data protection, Transparency and interpretability, Reproducibility and robustness, Intellectual property and ownership, Accountability and responsibility, Social impact and job displacement, Dual use and misuse*" (Abbadia, J.,2023). In the knowledge that the findings of all this research will need to be significantly amplified by digital media, making use of languages with a large audience for diversified communication.

6. Conclusion.

The aim of research is to shed more light on and update old information, to bring new discoveries, hypotheses and theories to light, in order to raise the level of science and better understand the world around us. This means increasing, enriching and/or clarifying our knowledge.

References

Abbadia, J. (2023, 06 27). *mindthegraph.com.* Retrieved from WWW.mindthegraph.com: https://mindthegraph.com/blog/fr/ai-dans-la-recherche-
universitaire/#:~:text=Elle%20peut%20automatiser%20les%20t%C3%A2ches, m%C3%AAme% 20la%20r%C3%A9daction%20de%20manuscrits.

Berry, M. (2023, January). *General Interest Periodicals-France.* Retrieved from www.proquest.com: https://www.proquest.com/newspapers/la-recherche-en-gestion-doit-
escapeaux/

Crié, D., al. (2022, 05 02). *lejdd.fr.* Retrieved from www.lejdd.fr: https://www.lejdd.fr/Societe/defiance-desinformation-pourquoi-lopposition-au-vaccin-anti- covid-continue-malgre-la-levee-du-passe-4109032

Ferrand, F. (2018, January 08). *europe1.fr.* Retrieved from www.europe1.fr: https://www.europe1.fr/emissions/Aujourd-hui-dans-l-Histoire/8-janvier-1642-la-mort-de- galileo-galilei-dit-galilee-3539747

Grawitz, M., & Al., &. (1994). Méthodes des sciences sociales, Paris. *L'Homme et la société Année*, pp. 111-112; 198-199.

Madeleine Grawitz (n.d.).

Mialaret, G. (2004). Finalités générales de la recherche scientifique. *Presses Universitaires de France*, 18-21.

Müller-Bloch, C. &. (2014). Framework for Rigorously Identifying Research Gaps in Qualitative Literature Reviews, The Thirty Sixth International Conference on Information Systems, Fort Worth. *Framework for Rigorously Identifying Research Gaps in Qualitative Literature Reviews,,* 1-19.

Müller-Bloch, C. &. (2015). A framework for rigorously identifying research gaps in qualitative literature reviews. *A framework for rigorously identifying research gaps in qualitative literature reviews*, 1-19.

Identifying the benefits of adopting triangulation in research

1. Introduction

The history of triangulation dates back to the 15th century, an approach invented by Renaissance mathematician, architect and painter ***Leon Battista Alberti,*** who was one of the first to demonstrate an illustrative method for determining distant distances. The aim of this study was to define the distance between two points using Thales' theory. (futura- sciences.com, 2023)

Nonetheless, this first triangular approach was flawed in terms of validity and reliability, as it could not corroborate with the planet's spherical shape.

To this day, an update of the aforementioned theory has been made by the famous "***Mathematician*** **Legendre**" who, thanks to his update, we can observe the development of satellites and radars, and this favours the analysis of distances in a much less approximate way, but triangulation remains the foundation of all summary distance reasoning.

To this end, the expansion of this approach to our era of triangulation is seen by researchers as a way of *"implementing multiple approaches to data collection for the study of social phenomena. The multiple methods approach thus attempts to understand the complexity of problems by studying them from more than one point of view."* (Sawadogo, 2020).

From the foregoing, we will pinpoint the benefits of triangulation on the main lines of research that constituted the points of improvement leading to the evolutionary theories of triangulation through the following steps.

2. Advantages of triangulation.

The purpose of triangulation is to determine the validity of knowledge acquired through research, since validity and scientificity are intrinsically linked to triangulation.

This exercise pits different investigative methods against each other to promote the stability and accuracy of the analyses carried out, and to compensate for the shortcomings of each approach by merging data from different collection tools in order to guarantee the reliability of the results (Savoie-Zajc, 1996b).

In this way, the results obtained can be used to corroborate data collected from separate sources, simplifying the effect of both systematic and random deviations that may occur in one of these studies.

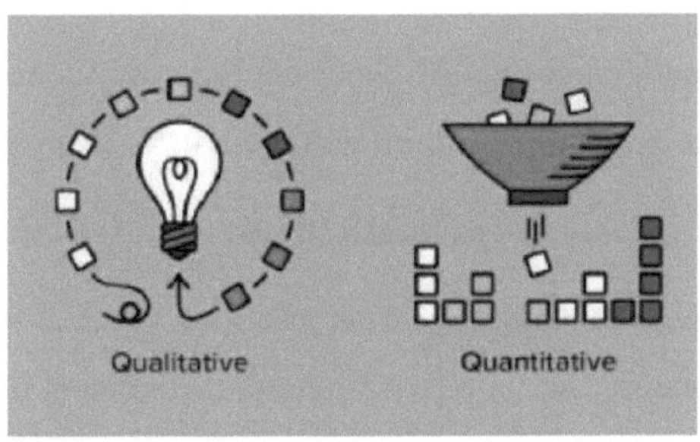

Necessarily based on pre-existing data sources (quantitative approach), triangulation enables rapid understanding a phenomenon and simplifies decision-making in a timely and appropriate manner.

Let's remember that the triangulation approach takes advantage of the different privileges of the approaches to achieve greater detail and depth in the data analysis (***qualitative***), in order to have a balanced distribution (***constructive***) and sample size, and to distinguish the socio-demographic characteristics of the respondents (***quantitative***), thus breaking the gap between the weaknesses in each of the approaches by complementing the other.

2.1. Advantages of qualitative triangulation

Combining qualitative research with the triangulation approach offers a number of advantages, providing researchers with a comprehensive analysis and assessment of the phenomenon under study, since the researcher himself is a key player in the questions posed during the study. But it also consolidates and reinforces the validity and credibility of the research results, through the confrontation of reliable expected results. In addition, it helps to overcome the limitations of any data source or methodology approached in a singular manner. (fastercapital.com, 2023)

To illustrate, triangulation using a qualitative research approach can take the form of an experimental study of the human resources management of a well-defined establishment in a specific sector with a societal impact. To achieve this, the researcher may use discussion forums and interviews to gain a fuller understanding of the beneficiaries' concerns, by comparing them with their expectations, in line with existing research in the culture of this environment.

2.2. Advantages of quantitative triangulation

Unlike qualitative triangulation, which is subjective in nature, quantitative triangulation makes use of large-scale digitized statistical data, which can facilitate analysis of various variables in record time, at low cost, using pre-existing ***(historical)*** data stored in databases or based on documentation in libraries.

This examination is carried out using interviews, observation and *focus groups.* It should be noted that the objectivity of the quantitative approach commonly makes its results more precise than those of the qualitative method. This is due to its specificity, which focuses on the processing and analysis of certain research questions, and makes it possible to predict certain behaviors. (en.surveymonkey.com, 2024).

2.3. Advantages of Mixed Method triangulation.

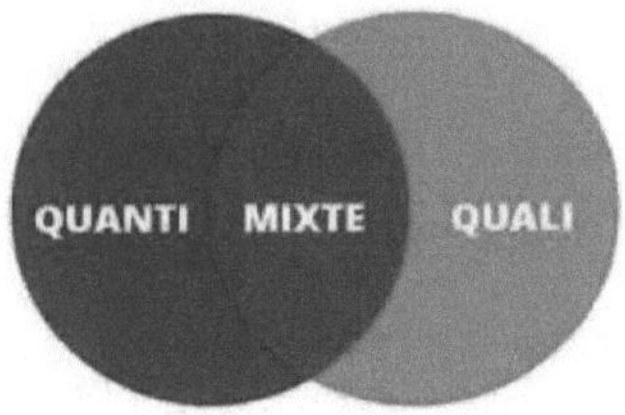

Before starting a research study, it is particularly important to determine the relative priority of each type of data in the event of conflicting results. And in the case of the mixed-methods approach, conceptions may vary according to the level of integration of the qualitative and quantitative.

And mixed method triangulation consists of merging the qualitative method with the quantitative method, based on the quantitative data using an identification sheet.

With this method we aim to take advantage of the multiple benefits of both approaches:

- more depth more detail.
- the sample size.

By simplifying the weaknesses of each through the complementarity of the other, the validity of the study can be strengthened if the research results are corroborated.

However, there are drawbacks in terms of resource consumption and the inability of one data collection to inform the other (Halcomb and Andrew, 2009).

3. Methodological gaps in triangulation

From a methodological point of view, based on our cross-sectional review of triangulation, we have pinpointed a number of methodological shortcomings that make the use of triangulation cumbersome, including the non-existence of a common formula that can be applied to all approaches.

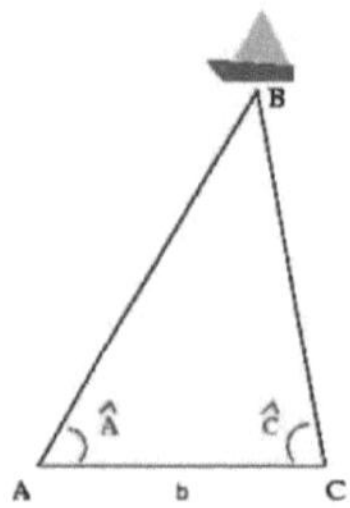

We can also underline the onerous nature of this exercise, which results in data being collected separately, sometimes with conflicting results. Authors Halcomb and Andrew point out that these types of gaps take ' longer to complete and, above all, vary according to the priority of the data collected, whether quantitative or qualitative. On the other hand, when triangulation is applied to explanatory analyses, researchers use quantitative (existing) data

It should be noted that research studies require the identification of resource people with the necessary skills likely to advance the research project in general, and in particular for academic research, they require a good number of the skills needed in view of the time constraint that ethical requirements in project management require. *"financial resources/costs, time and data management"* (Halcomb and Andrew, 2009).

Indeed, as Edyburn (1999) points out, *"the era of the isolated researcher in his workshop now seems to be definitively over. Research now relies more often than not on increasingly inter-university, interdisciplinary and international teams."*

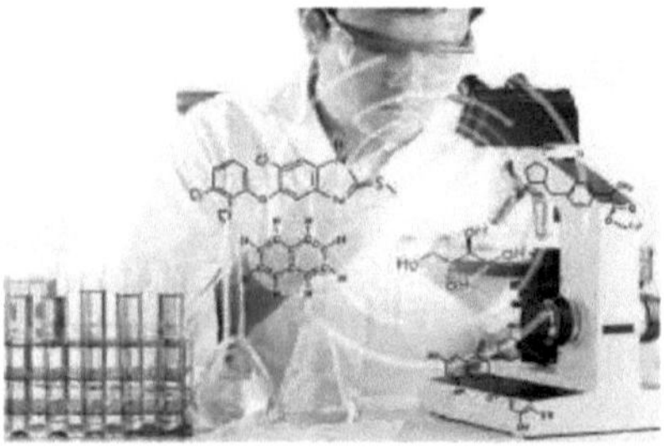

From the very beginnings of modern science, the dangers of science without conscience and the need for "*research ethics*" have been emphasized (Conseil national du développement des SHS, (2001) and so there's nothing radically new about this notion. We find that researchers have difficulty in aligning themselves with ethical requirements, and they struggle to provide us with a clear, well-developed audit trail, as well as detailed explanations of decisions taken throughout the research process, which remains a major challenge to researchers in getting their work published.

4. Triangulation improvement points.

Nowadays, with the evolution of the Internet and the daily use of its functionalities, in particular NICT and AI, the combination of human faculties with the performance of machines and their components enables the absorption and interpretation of big data in record time, facilitates compound decision-making, and allows large-scale data collection and storage:

- *"Computer systems;*
- *Data with management systems;*
- *Advanced AI algorithms (code)."*

In order to reduce the gap between the results generated by these tools, they need a sufficient amount of information from the human being, given their speed of analysis and information processing. (netapp.com, 2024)

In conclusion, the use of new information and communication technologies (NICTs) and Artificial Intelligence (AI) is revolutionizing the world of scientific research through increased communication and collaboration, making them an integral part of the scientific research process in the current era.

References

Andrew, S., & Halcomb, E. J. (2009). *Mixed methods research for nursing and the health sciences, London; England, Wiley-Blackwell.* Retrieved from www.wiley.com : https://www.wiley.com/en-br/Mixed+Methods+Research+for+Nursing+and+the+Health+Sciences-p-9781405167772

Conseil national du développement des SHS, . (2001). IV. L'éthique de la recherche en sciences humaines et sociales. In: Conseil national du développement des SHS, Pour une politique des sciences de l'Homme et de la société: Recueil des travaux (1998-2000). *Presses Universitaires de France Paris cedex 14*, 93-114.

Edyburn, D. L. (1999). *go.gale.com.* Retrieved from www.go.gale.com: https://go.gale.com/ps/i.do?id=GALE%7CA100878432&sid=googleScholar&v=2.1&it=r&linka ccess=abs&issn=07319487&p=AONE&sw=w&userGroupName=anon%7E9d3 8a91b&aty=ope n-web-entryfastercapital.com. (2023, December 12). *fastercapital.com.* Retrieved from www.fastercapital.com: https://fastercapital.com/fr/contenu/Triangulation--renforcement-des-resultats-de-l-analyse-qualitative.html#:~:text=There%20are%20four%20principal%20types,several%20sources%20of%20data%C3%A9es%20for

en.surveymonkey.com. (2024). *en.surveymonkey.com.* Retrieved from www.fr.surveymonkey.com: https://fr.surveymonkey.com/mp/quantitative-vs-qualitative-research/

futura-sciences.com. (2023). *futura-sciences.com.* Retrieved from www.futura-sciences.com: https://www.futura-sciences.com/planete/definitions/geographie-geodesie-4429/

netapp.com. (2024). *netapp.com*. Retrieved from www.netapp.com: https://www.netapp.com/fr/artificial-intelligence/what-is-artificial-intelligence/

Sawadogo, H. P. (2020, February). les logiques sociales de la pratique de la mendicité par des mères de jumeaux dans la ville de Ouagadougou. Quebec City, Quebec, Canada.

Actions to be taken to maintain confidentiality, integrity, etc. by researchers

1. Introduction

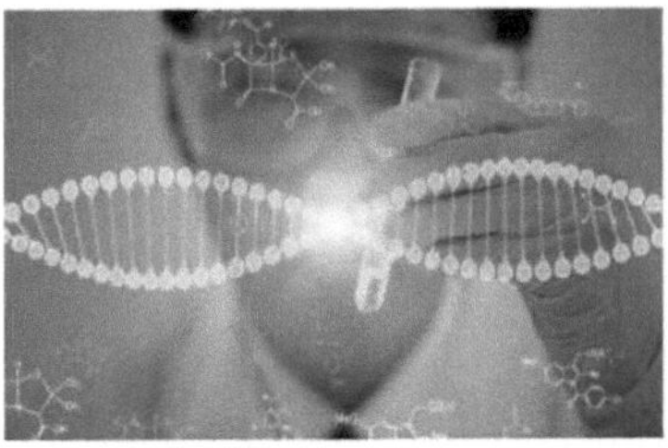

Since the dawn of time, from anthropological studies (*natural sciences*) to the digital age and the advent of Artificial Intelligence (AI), the concern for securing participants in scientific research has always been at the heart of scholars.

To this end, a regulatory body has been set up, charged with pursuing life-saving interests and also acting as a jurisdiction for approval and ethics applications. This body is responsible for safeguarding the psychological and physical integrity, as well as the rights, of those involved in research, with a view to guiding and orienting the various fields of research.

It should be pointed out that this process is an imperative for any researcher, as it is indeed a metaphysical stance relating to the consented participation of the human being (the respondent) in the study based on a free and informed choice as specified in 2018 by Lambert-Chan, M. in her article ***"A Student's Little Survival Guide"***, which states: *"As soon as we do research involving human beings, we need the assent of a research ethics committee (REC) before proceeding with the recruitment of participants"* (Lambert-Chan, M., 2018).

It's worth mentioning that, in the current context, the ethical values of scientific research and technoscience have a technological outcome, while the latter downplays the imperative nature of ethics, making the latter an adjunct in the research process at the risk of causing harmful consequences for mankind. In order not to fail in its research mission, the ethics committee should promote a generational transition of ethical values, but maintain an authentic approach with the aim of ensuring that ethical questioning remains at the heart of the scientific process and work, and not at the heart of its activity, in order to guarantee the confidentiality and protection of respondents. As proposed by (Larochelle, Y., 2007).

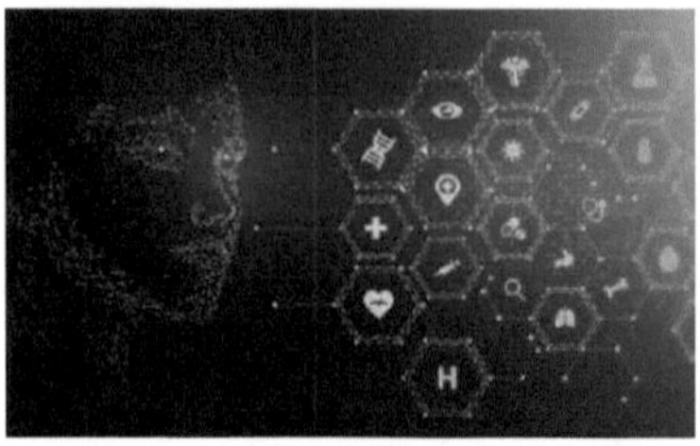

Over the years, a number of questionable scientific experiments have been carried out on people, with no regard for their consent, their vulnerability or their psychological state. (disabled, ill, minor, etc.).

Referring to Balzac's famous quote from the 19th century: "You can't make an omelette without breaking eggs", the author used this figurative language to mean that nothing is achieved without sacrifice, i.e. that there is inevitably collateral damage involved in every result. It's worth noting that there was a clear absence of scientific research ethics in this practice.

Around 5 centuries ago, Rabelais said that *"Science without conscience is but the ruin of the soul"...* and today Frédéric Vézard repeats this quotation in his editorial "***Aujourd'hui Le Parisien***", recommending that it be engraved in capital letters at the entrance to every scientific research laboratory (Frédéric, 2017).

With this in mind, our work will focus on the actions that must be taken by researchers to comply with the ethical requirements laid down by the bodies responsible for guiding and censoring the conduct of research, aimed at guaranteeing data protection and ensuring the anonymity *(confidentiality)* of respondents and the investigator.

In view of the technological revolution and the advent of AI *(artificial intelligence),* data collection, security and participant security require extreme rigor, based on the protocol drawn up by the Comité d'éthique de reche, which we intend to contribute to the edifice.

2. Constituents of scientific research ethics.

The optimization of living conditions is at the heart of the morality of progress, and the evolution of science must have a benevolent character for mankind, since scientific progress goes hand in hand with universal well-being in many respects:

- **Beneficence**: the aim of research ethics is to enable researchers to do no harm to participants, while increasing benefits and minimizing drawbacks as far as possible. Bearing in mind that beneficence is linked to the principle of utility, the ethics commission, after an in-depth analysis and censorship of the risks involved in the research subject, draws up recommendations aimed at protecting the investigator and the respondents, which is the guarantee of non-maleficence.

As Delfosse puts it: *"the quality of an action is measured by its near or distant consequences on the whole of individual and social life".*

Non-maleficence: Deriving its essence from the principle of ***beneficence*** in research ethics, it owes its existence to the fact of measuring the risks concurred in during a scientific experiment, and this exercise takes place a few years later after the results of this scientific experiment have been made public

Its intervention is carried out retrospectively, with the aim of securing and measuring the impact that the research would have had, given that it is essential to know how to maintain a balance between the individual good and the collective good, and above all how to make them coexist without violating the rules of dignity or tainting the respect due to human beings (Delfosse, 1993).

- **Respect for people:** more than seventy-five years after the Universal Declaration of Human Rights, this question is worth its weight in gold, and requires us to reflect on this interrogation in order to determine whether ***"Do scientific advances jeopardize human dignity?"***an observation made in 2009 by Fiacat president Sylvie Bukhari-de Pontual*: "All international texts for the protection of human rights are based on the concept of human dignity. And yet dignity is constantly being trampled underfoot, with the development of genetics and science in general, for example.* "(Pontual, 2009) This reflection prompts us to review or readjust the ethical principles that serve as safeguards for scientific research in general and medical research in particular, with human dignity at the top of the pyramid.

Based on our theme, the human being at the heart of research must be considered as an end in itself and not used as a means to an end, as we see today, human dignity is increasingly desacralized in research. For it should be noted that science needs to exploit human potential in order to evolve, and this is sometimes at odds with the respect accorded to human beings. Jean-Claude Ameisen,

Chairman of Inserm's Ethics Committee, argues that: *"With science, there is a risk of reification and dehumanization, because science disregards the singularity of the individual. It treats us as objects, whereas we experience ourselves as subjects".* (Jean-Claude, 2008). Given that respect for human dignity is at great risk as a result of the evolution of teloscience, the research process must reflect fairness and justice.

- **Justice:** this principle emphasizes the aspect of equality (*simple probity*), which is supposed to be applied to all participants involved in the research. These must have the same prilleges, the choice to contribute to it in the same capacity. As requested by the World Health Organization (WHO, 2018). For health research, all participants must have the same equivalent resources for equal access to health. This is how it defines equity as: *"the absence of avoidable or remediable differences between different groups of people, whether defined according to social, economic, demographic or geographic criteria"* (Loignon, 2018).

Let's not forget that our cultural habits and laws have been turned upside down by the speed of technological progress, and the advent of digital technology. We tend to believe that the notion of data confidentiality is old hat, and yet according to a blog published in February 2020 by *the Vice President and Head of Risk, Legal and Administrative Affairs at the World Bank Group*, it's *"since 1918 that the first legally binding treaty on the protection of privacy and personal data has been signed".* (Tafara, 2020).

From the above, our contribution as researchers will take into account technological advances to further consolidate respect for human dignity and the effective application of existing rules on ethics in scientific or medical research. It's worth noting that there are many issues at stake in research, including *practical, intellectual and ethical issues*. As a result, we are taking steps today mainly to regulate and ensure the protection of the data in our possession, by paying the utmost attention to the processes of collecting, using, archiving and sharing personal information.

These issues serve as the fundamental pillars that guide researchers in carrying out their work and fulfilling their commitment.

We can note :

- **Reliability**: *this ensures the quality of the research, through careful analysis and efficient use of resources and methodology.*

- **Integrity**: this is *a factor that enables researchers to make their work known in a complete, objective and, above all, transparent way.*
- **Respect:** *participants, the environment, culture and society.*
- **Responsibility:** *tutoring and management of research-related activities, from initiative to publication of the theory, i.e. (organization, training, registration).*

3. Our contribution.

Our aim is to implement a policy that promotes a better balance between good ethical practice and minimizing the data confidentiality loopholes that accompany the digital era. To achieve this, scientific integrity is a means of encouraging and reminding researchers and research-promoting institutions of their commitment to scientific research.

As researchers, we can see that integrity is intrinsically linked to the notion of respect and human dignity in scientific research, like links in a long chain with the notion of confidentiality (privacy) in research.

The Swiss academies define integrity as :

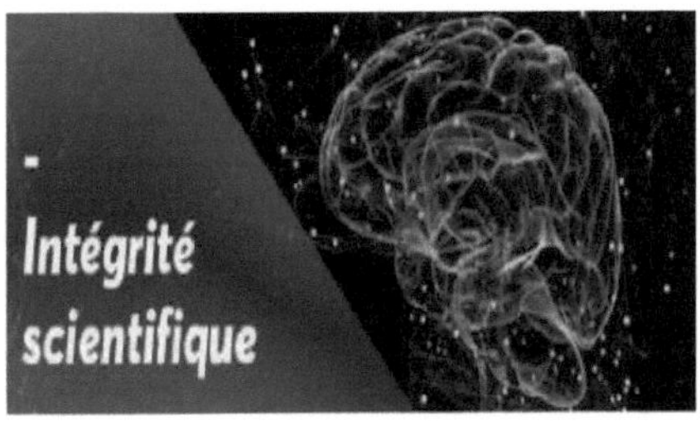

"Integrity is a high value of existence, both from an individual and social point of view. In the scientific context, integrity is the personal commitment of researchers to respect the rules of good scientific practice. Truthfulness and openness, self-discipline, self-criticism and righteousness are indispensable to behavior of integrity". From this definition we understand that integrity gives essence to research, so an attitude of integrity is indispensable for anyone enrolling in research activities. (academies-suisses.ch, 2008).

Having identified the threats to scientific research in our time, the Swiss academies, through their eminent Professors, have drawn up a *"Memoradum on Scientific Integrity"*, in which they emphasize that *"the constant increase in administrative tasks, lack of time, financial impasses and the pressure of competition, as well as social change, can encourage researchers to use dubious or illicit means to draw attention to their work and achieve rapid success"*. This is why, in response to this impending situation, a number of boundaries need to be drawn around scientific activities to reinforce their credibility.

References

Academies-suisses.ch. (2008). Integrity in scientific research Basic principles and procedures. *academies-suisses.ch*, 13-28. Retrieved from www.academies-suisses.ch,: www.academies-suisses.ch, info@akademien-schweiz.ch

Delfosse (1993). À la source des normes en éthique de la recherche. *Presses de l'Université de Montréal*, 51-72.

Frédéric, V. (2017, October 7). Science without conscience is but the ruin of the soul. paris, paris, france.

Jean-Claude, A. (2008). Human dignity endangered by advances in research. *La Croix.*

LAMBERT-CHAN, M. (2018, January 23). *books.openedition.org.* Retrieved from www.books.openedition.org: http://books.openedition.org/pum/7690

Larochelle, Y. (2007). Laval Ethics at the heart of the natural sciences? *Laval théologique et philosophique,* 561-575. https://doi.org/10.7202/018176ar .

Loignon, C. (2018). Equity in research. *ENGAGE.*

Pontual, S. B.-d. (2009). colloquium organized by the Institut catholique de Paris and the Commission Justice et Paix de l'épiscopat - dedicated to "human dignity. *colloquium organized by the Institut catholique de Paris and the Commission Justice et Paix de l'épiscopat - dedicated to "human dignity.* Paris.

Tafara, E. (2020, February 07). *worldbank.org.* Retrieved from www.worldbank.org: https://blogs.worldbank.org/fr/voices/proteger-la-confidentialite-donnees-numeriques

Staff remuneration policy in public health and quality of healthcare services in the DRC

1. Related literature

Remuneration for any work performed remains important. As the saying goes, *"All work deserves pay"*, which means that remuneration is a complex set of "*concrete, intangible, variable and even emotional*" benefits.

This isn't just a paycheck. **Rakotozafy, J P,** supports the complexity of this saying by pointing out: *"That there are sorrows that deserve generosity. Pay is not just expressed in terms of money. It could be a verbal recognition, an acceptance of the service rendered."* (linternaute.fr, 2019).

In order to meet the requirements of fairness, honesty and transparency, the DRC has revised upwards its budget for the payment of state civil servants. With the 2023 budget commitment plan published on its official website, the first institution's allocations have grown by around 20% of the 2024 annual budget, as analyzed by actualite.cd (www.actualite.cd, 2024).

In April 2022, Lihau J.P., *Minister of the Civil Service*, announced a 30% increase in income for all civil servants. But also a downward revision of the professional income tax (IPR) from 15% to 3% for both the private and public sectors (www.radiookapi.net, 2022).

Despite this progress, the concern about the SMIG in the DRC is linked to the country's economic situation. This is because the SMIG has always been set in local currency (the Congolese franc), whose value is constantly depreciating as a result of political, economic and sometimes legal events.

Failure to respect the SMIG legal value becomes a real headache between employers and agents, with one setting working conditions and the other imposing strict respect for his rights (Juslain, 2020).

These facts do not leave the health sector on the sidelines, as demonstrated in 2022 by researchers Mikonge, T., et al. On the question: "*Rémunération de personnel de l'Hôpital Général de Référence de Bagira : zone de santé de la république démocratique du Congo*" this study aimed to improve the social well-being of health workers in return for their salaries.

The result of this analysis is that the remuneration of "*HGR/Bagira*" agents was established according to level and/or tier, with the range of participants receiving a suffering salary. With these facts, the researchers establish that remuneration difficulties still persist in healthcare establishments

This is worth the weight of gold of our research, with a view to enlightening political decision-makers, economic operators, as well as representatives of community strata, with a view to reaching the right resolutions.

2. Research deviations

With regard to our research topic, we have pinpointed the discrepancies between the literature and the size of the population that benefits from the advances made in the remuneration of state employees, i.e. 1,450 *million civil servants,* 350 *thousand of whom are likely to retire. (actualite.cd, 2021)*

An observation noting a salary increase of around 36% at the country's leading institution, let us note that the said increase remains unpaid following currency depreciation, a consequence linked to the lack of a fundamental financial study made in this sense, and the impact is that decisions taken to this end pass for populist speeches to the underserved societal stratum (actualite.cd, 2024).

Still in the same chapter, concerning the methodological approach, the collection tools used reflect neither the validity nor the reliability of the results, making them neither credible nor transferable.

The budget allocated to this sector is progressing at a snail's pace: from 2009 to 2019, the allocated budget was 0.29% and has only evolved by a margin of 0.30% over this decade. An increase of up to 3% is expected for this sector in the 2024 budget year (ACP, 2023).

Microsoft
Excel 2016

3. **Search method**

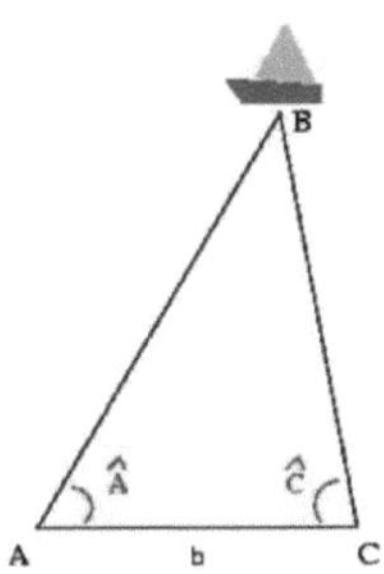

Given the complexity of our study, we have opted for the triangulation method. This choice is justified by the following strategic reasons: the aim is to benefit from both approaches:

- *The sample size is crucial to capture the socio-demographic characteristics of respondents via a structured form (simple random probabilistic) for reliable, credible and valid statistical data ensuring non-refutable (quantitative) transferability.*

- *Determine how respondents and interviewers subjectively perceive the phenomenon under study* (fastercapital.com, 2023).

- *Demonstrably, this method facilitates the experimental analysis of management resources (human, financial, material, temporal, etc.) in a sector with a precise social impact (qualitative).*

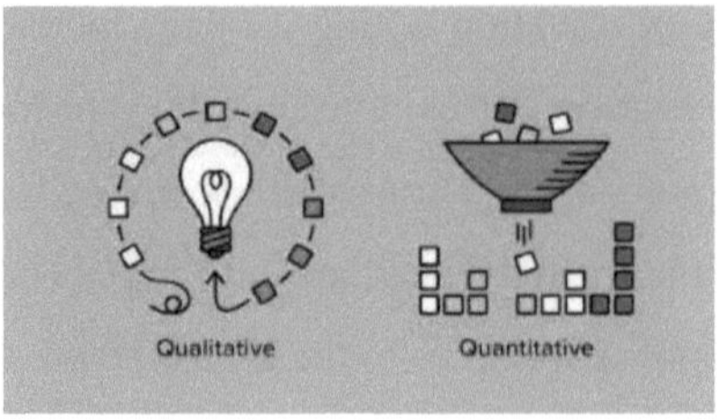

Based on the evidence listed above, our choice stems from the compensatory nature of this method, which favors a palliation of all types of discrepancies observed by combining the results of different tools (Baribeau & Chantal Royer, 2012).

4. Possible sampling biases

For this study, it should be noted that response and non-response biases are likely to be encountered. To remedy this, the questions used to create the structured form essentially require anonymity in order to avoid any subjectivity and any form of influence on the respondents.

Given that data collection will take place in strict compliance with ethical standards (anonymity...) guaranteeing the privacy of the researcher and participants to avoid any form of pressure on them and avoid compliance bias (voxco.com, 2023).

5. Guaranteeing ethical standards

the concern for the safety of participants in scientific research has always been at the heart of scholarly endeavors.

Thus, ethical considerations during research remain at the heart of many discussions aimed at establishing the researcher's responsibility, and guaranteeing the physical and psychological integrity and privacy of the investigator and participants, before, during and after investigations.

It is for the aforementioned evidences that any thematic must go through a Research Ethics Committee (REC) because when a research involves human beings, the researcher needs an assent from the committee (Lambert-Chan, M., 2018).

In this day and age, the spin-offs of telescience and scientific research have technological outlets, while these advances reduce the absoluteness of ethical values. To quote Delfosse: *"the consequences of an action, whether near or far, influence the quality of individual and social life"*. (Delfosse, 1993).

References

Actualite.cd. (2021, October 6). [News article]. Retrieved from https://actualite.cd/2021/10/06/rdc-avec-1450000-fonctionnaires-et-un-nombre-important-des- fictifs-jp-lihau-dit-militer

Actualite.cd. (2024, March 7). [News article]. Retrieved from https://actualite.cd/2024/03/07/rdc-avec-une-augmentation-de-pres-de-20-de-son-budget-annuel- en-2024-la-presidence-de- la

ACP. (2023, August 29). [Nation article]. Retrieved from http s ://acp. cd/nation/la-rdc-ambiti onne- de-consacrer-3-du-budget-2024-a-linnovation-technologique/

Baribeau, C. and Royer, C. (2012). L'entretien individuel en recherche qualitative: usages et modes de présentation dans la Revue des sciences de l'éducation. *Revue des sciences de l'éducation* , 38(1), 23-45. Retrieved from https://www.erudit.org/en/journals/rse/2012-v38-n1- rse0675/1016748ar/

Quickcapital.com. (2023, December 12). [Content article]. Retrieved from https://fastercapital.com/fr/contenu/Triangulation--renforcement-des-resultats-de-l-analyse-qualitative.html#:~:text=There%20are%20four%20principal%20types,several%types,several%types,several%types,several%types,several%types,several%types,several%types,several%types. 20sources%20de%20donn%C3%A9es%20pour

Juslain, New Brunswick (2020). [Review article]. Retrieved from https://www.nomos- elibrary.de/10.5771/2363-6262-2020-2-299.pdf

Linternaute.fr. (2019, February 7). [Proverb]. Retrieved from https://www.linternaute.fr/proverbe/705/toute-peine-merite-salaire/

Radiookapi.net. (2022, April 20). [Political article]. Retrieved from https://www.radiookapi.net/2022/04/20/actualite/politique/rdc-le-gouvernement-augmente-de- 30-the-base-salary-of-des

Voxco.com. (2023). [Blog post]. Retrieved from https://www.voxco.com/fr/blog/types-de- biais-de-reponse-comment-les-eviter/

Ethics and social responsibility corporate strategy

Summary

This article explores the growing impact of *"ethics and corporate social responsibility"* (CSR) in corporate policies, in the face of rising stakeholder expectations for ethical behavior and positive contributions to society. It analyzes the main conceptual frameworks of CSR, such as party theory, shared value creation and fair trade, which shed light on the complex interventions between organizations and society.

It then examines the ethics and CSR management tools and mechanisms used by companies. These include codes of conduct, mission and values statements, ethical training programs, integrated risk management, stakeholder consultation, sustainability auditing and accounting, as well as the use of advanced technologies such as data analysis and artificial intelligence.

The article highlights the importance of holistically integrating these tools and mechanisms into overall industry policy. It also highlights persistent challenges, such as measuring impact, managing complex ethical dilemmas and adapting to evolving societal expectations.

In addition, companies that commit to an ethical and truly responsible approach can position themselves as key players in sustainability and equity, contributing to a more sustainable and equitable world. Constant adaptation, innovation and the implementation of responsible practices are essential to guarantee the long-term success of companies in a changing economic and societal context.

Keywords: Ethics; CSR; Corporate strategy development

1. Introduction

In the current economic context, the integration of ethics and CSR has become an imperative for modern corporate strategies. Companies face growing expectations from their stakeholders for ethical behavior and a positive contribution to society (Carroll & Brown, 2018).

This article examines the various tools and mechanisms used by companies to manage ethics and CSR, as well as conceptual frameworks for understanding exchanges between business and society.

2. CSR theories and conceptual frameworks

Stakeholder theory, originally developed by (Freeman, 1984), remains a fundamental conceptual framework for understanding interactions between business and society. According to this theory, companies have responsibilities towards a wide range of stakeholders, beyond just shareholders (Freeman et al., 2020). This approach leads to a more holistic view of corporate performance, adopting a more comprehensive approach to performance, which takes ESG aspects into account.

The concept of "shared value creation" proposed by (Porter & Kramer, 2019) suggests that companies can simultaneously create economic and societal value by identifying and exploiting the points of intersection between their activities and society's needs. This perspective offers a means of reconciling profit objectives with the imperatives of social responsibility.

"Fair trade" has evolved to encompass not only fair trade practices in global supply chains, but also broader considerations to promote fairness and sustainability in all their operations. (Raynolds, 2018).

"Green alliances" represent strategic partnerships between companies, NGOs and other parties aimed at promoting environmental sustainability (Wassmer & al., 2017).

2.1. Tools and mechanisms for promoting ethics and CSR within the company.

✓ **Mission and value statements:** Mission and value statements contain the fundamental purpose and principles that guide the organization's actions. Recent research has shown that well-written, authentic mission and value statements can propel the company towards better ethical and financial performance (Chun & al.,

2019). To be effective, these statements must reflect a genuine driver for change in the company's culture and practices.

✓ **Codes of ethics:** Codes of ethics are a formalized set of rules and ethical principles that an organization's employees and managers are required to respect.

✓ According to (Kaptein, 2019), the most effective codes are those that are specific to the particularities of the company and its market, rather than generic documents. The effectiveness of a code of ethics largely depends on its implementation, which requires clear communication, regular training and visible commitment from management (Trevino & al., 2020).

✓ **Reporting and counseling methods:** Communication and counseling mechanisms are essential to the effective management of ethics and CSR within companies. Ethics hotlines, in particular, provide a space for employees to report safe ethical concerns without fear of reprisal. Research by (Lee & Xiao, 2018) reveals that companies that equip themselves with effective, easy-to-access helplines record stronger financial results and a healthier corporate culture. These channels present transparency and trust, empowering employees to safely report unethical behavior.

✓ **Climate risk assessment:** With the growing focus on climate change, many companies are now integrating climate risk assessment into their overall risk management process. A study by (Kouloukoui, Christopoulos, & Tsoumas, 2019) highlighted the importance of this practice for engaging in a transition to more sustainable and climate-resilient operations.

✓ **Integrated risk management**: more and more companies are adopting a collaborative approach to risk management, involving all departments of the company that integrates ethical and CSR risks alongside traditional financial, operational and strategic risks. According to a study by (Flage, & Aven, 2015), this approach provides a better understanding of the interconnections between different types of risk, and enables more strategic and informed decision-making.

✓ **Advanced technologies:** AI and data analytics are opening up new avenues for more responsible and sustainable ethics and CSR management. These tools make it possible to identify and analyze risks more thoroughly and anticipatively. AI can automate the analysis of big data and provide predictive insights, while data analytics can more accurately quantify environmental impacts and stakeholder behaviors. A study by (Scherer, 2016) highlights the ability of these technologies to identify hidden trends.

✓ However, the use of AI and data analytics raises crucial ethical issues. It is essential to ensure responsible and transparent use of these technologies, respecting privacy and leading to discrimination. Integrating these technologies into ethical management and CSR offers significant potential for industries committed to a responsible and sustainable approach.

✓ **Ethics education and training:** To embed ethics and CSR in daily practices, it is essential to train employees in these concepts and equip them to make ethical decisions. Recent research highlights the importance of formal, ongoing and tailored training programs (Warren & al., 2014), complemented by e-learning approaches (Trevino et al., 2020). The integration of ethical considerations into function-specific training (Schwartz, 2018) and the use of ethical dilemmas are effective practices. Training programs adapt to the specific needs of senior managers and the integration of new employees (Kaptein, 2019). Regular assessment of plan productivity and promotion of a culture of continuous learning are essential to embed ethics in organizational culture.

✓ **Stakeholder consultation and partnerships:** Stakeholder consultation and partnership development have become key elements of ethical management and CSR. (Freudenreich, Gond, & Mourrain, 2020) emphasize the importance of proactive and continuous stakeholder engagement to improve sustainability performance. (Civera, Mele, & Schrempf-Stirling, 2019) propose an engagement assessment framework based on transparency, inclusiveness and responsiveness.

- ✓ Consultation methods vary, with a trend towards more collaborative approaches (Testa & al., 2018). Strategic partnerships, particularly with civil society, are crucial to tackling complex sustainability challenges (Dentoni & al., 2018; van Tulder & Keen, 2018).

- ✓ However, ethical considerations remain, such as the risk of manipulation of the parties involved (Crane & al., 2019) and power imbalances in partnerships (H0vring, 2017).

- ✓ **Auditing, accounting and reporting:** Ethics and CSR auditing, accounting and reporting have evolved considerably in recent years. (Mion & Loza Adaui, 2019) note an accumulated standardization of CSR reports, improving their comparability.

(Stubbs & Higgins, 2018) highlight the emergence of integrated reporting for a holistic view of value creation. (Boiral, Cornelissen, & Maignan, 2019) identifying challenges in non-financial information assurance. (Schaltegger & Burritt, 2017) propose a framework for sustainability accounting, while (Bebbington, & Unerman, 2018) explore its role in achieving the SDGs.

(Michelon, Delmas, & Hoffman, 2020) Highlight persistent problems of information quality and reliability. Regulatory initiatives such as the European NFRD directive aim to improve transparency and corporate responsibility in CSR.

3. Conclusion

Ethics and CSR have become essential elements of long-term corporate success. By integrating these considerations into their overall strategy, companies can not only improve their positioning and strengthen their trust capital, but also achieve value creation that meets the needs of all. The ethics and CSR landscape is constantly evolving, requiring continuous adaptation and innovation. Companies that make a genuine commitment in this direction will be able to position themselves as responsible players and contribute to a more sustainable and equitable world.

References

Bebbington, , J., & Unerman, J. (2018). *Sustainability accounting and reporting.* Routledge.

Boiral, , O., Cornelissen,, T., & Maignan,, I. (2019). an emerging field. Journal of Business Ethics. *Sustainability reporting assurance 158 (3)*, 575-596.

Carroll,, A., & Brown,, S. (2018). *Business and society: ethics, sustainability and stakeholder management.* Pearson Education.

Chun,, RY, , Lee,, Park, , CW, , & Chung,, N. (2019). The role of mission statement and value statement in corporate ethical behavior. *Journal of Business Ethics 155 (3)*, 623-643.

Civera,, P., Mele,, D., & Schrempf-Stirling,, J. (2019). A stakeholder engagement framework for corporate sustainability. *Business Strategy and the Environment , 28 (8)*, 1472-1486.

Crane,, A., Matten,, D., & Glozer,, S. (2019). *Business ethics: managing corporate citizenship and sustainability in the 21st century* . Oxford University Press.

Dentoni,, D., Gômez-Me^a,, LR,, & Nunez-Nickel,, M. (2018). The future of corporate social responsibility . *Business Horizons , 61 (1)*, 47-56.

Flage,, R., & Aven,, T. (2015). Integrating ethical risks into integrated risk management: a framework for assessing and managing ethical risks. *Journal of Business Ethics , 129 (1)*, 21-34.

Freeman, R. (1984). *Strategic management: a partnership approach.* Pitman.

Freeman,, RE,, Harrison,, JS,, Wicks,, AC,, . . . BL. (2020). Stakeholder theory: the state of the art. . *Journal of Management Studies , 57 (1)*, , 1-23.

Freudenreich,, H., Gond,, J.-P., & Mourrain,, J.-M. (2020). Corporate sustainability and stakeholder engagement: critical review and research agenda. *Journal of Business Ethics , 164 (2)*, 235-253.

H0vring, P. (2017). Corporate social responsibility and power relations: a critical analysis. *Business Ethics Quarterly , 27 (2)*, 191-218.

Kaptein, M. (2019). *Codes of conduct: a practical guide to developing and implementing ethical guidelines* . Routledge.

Kouloukoui, A., Christopoulos, D., & Tsoumas, C. (2019). Climate change risk assessment in the energy sector: a review of existing frameworks. *Energy Policy 132* , 43-58.

Lee, J., & Xiao, J. (2018). The impact of ethical hotline on financial performance: evidence from Chinese listed companies. *Journal of Business Ethics , 152 (4)*, 807-820.

Michelon, G., Delmas, M., & Hoffman, A. (2020). The accuracy and completeness of sustainability reporting: a meta-analysis of existing research. *Journal of Business Ethics , 162 (1)*, 137-160.

Mion, S., & Loza Adaui, C. (2019). Corporate social responsibility reporting: a literature review. *Journal of Business Ethics 157 (4)*, 969-997.

Porter, M., & Kramer, M. (2019). *Creating shared value: how to reinvent capitalism and unleash a wave of innovation and growth.* Harvard Business Review Press.

Raynolds, L. (2018). *Fair trade: the movement, the market and the future.* Cornell University Press.

Schaltegger, S., & Burritt, R. (2017). *Sustainability accounting and reporting.* Routledge.

Scherer, A. (2016). Big data and ethical decision-making: the use of artificial intelligence in business ethics. *Journal of Business Ethics 134 (2)*, 245-257.

Schwartz, M. (2018). *Corporate social responsibility: a managerial perspective.* Routledge.

Stubbs, W., & Higgins, C. (2018). *Integrated reporting: a guide to creating value* . John Wiley & Sons.

Testa, F., Conti, F., & Di Vaio, A. (2018). Corporate social responsibility and stakeholder engagement: a systematic literature review. *Sustainability , 10 (10)*, 3693.

Trevino, LK, Brown, ME, Hartman, & LP. (2020). *Managing ethics in the workplace: an integrated approach.* Wiley.

van Tulder, R., & Keen, M. (2018). *Global business and sustainability.* Routledge.

Warren, DA, Snell, SA, Chen, & PY. (2014). *Ethics in business: a guide to decision making* . Pearson Education.

Wassmer, R., Pacheco, PAA, Lopes, & AG. (2017). Green alliances: a review and research agenda. *Journal of Cleaner Production , 142*, 3417-3430.

General conclusion

This collection of research articles concludes by highlighting the crucial and interconnected role of ethical considerations and robust methodologies in ensuring the validity, reliability and societal impact of research efforts. The diverse studies presented, covering methodological approaches, ethical frameworks and real-world applications, converge on the overarching message that responsible research is not simply a matter of adhering to guidelines, but rather a fundamental commitment to intellectual integrity and social justice.

The recurring theme of methodological pluralism highlights the limits of using singular approaches to answer complex research questions. The articles convincingly demonstrate that the integration of qualitative and quantitative methods, coupled with techniques such as triangulation, greatly enhances the richness and robustness of research results. This approach recognizes the inherent complexities of social phenomena and the need to take into account multiple perspectives to achieve a more nuanced and comprehensive understanding. The continuing advocacy of mixed-method approaches reflects a move away from simplistic methodological dichotomies towards a more sophisticated and pragmatic understanding of research design.

Moreover, the emphasis on ethical considerations goes beyond mere compliance with regulations. The articles systematically underline the profound responsibility of researchers in protecting the welfare and rights of participants. Informed consent, data confidentiality and avoidance of bias are consistently highlighted as paramount concerns, reflecting a growing awareness of the potential for harm, direct and indirect, arising from research practices. Exploring the ethical dilemmas associated with emerging technologies, such as AI, highlights the urgent need for adaptive, forward-looking ethical guidelines that respond to new challenges and mitigate potential harms.

The case study on remuneration policies in the public health sector in the DRC convincingly illustrates the concrete consequences of methodological and ethical shortcomings. It demonstrates the profound impact that inadequate research design, limited access to resources and insufficient ethical considerations can have on vulnerable populations. The study underlines that responsible research is not just an academic exercise, but a crucial instrument for promoting social justice and making a significant contribution to improving human life.

In conclusion, this collection of articles successfully demonstrates the critical interplay between methodological rigor and ethical considerations in the development of responsible research practices. By highlighting the limits of simplistic approaches, emphasizing the crucial role of ethical frameworks and illustrating the real impact of research decisions, these studies provide valuable information for researchers, policy-makers and anyone wishing to contribute to the production of knowledge in an ethical and responsible manner. The diverse perspectives presented ultimately underscore the need for an ongoing commitment to critical self-reflection, methodological sophistication and an unwavering dedication to the highest standards of ethical conduct in all research endeavors.

Table of contents

Summary 1

Introduction 3

Identifying research gaps for future research future research 5

1. Introduction 6
3. Anglophone approach. 7
4. Gaps in research. 8
5. Research implications for the future. 9
6. Conclusion. 11

References 12

Identifying the benefits of adopting triangulation in research 13

1. Introduction 14
2. Advantages of triangulation 15
3. Methodological gaps in triangulation 17
4. Triangulation improvement points. 19

References 20

Actions to be taken to maintain confidentiality, integrity, etc. by researchers 22

1. Introduction 23
2. Constituents of scientific research ethics. 25
3. Our contribution. 29

References 31

Staff remuneration policy in public health and quality of healthcare services in the DRC 32

1. Related literature 33
2. Research deviations 34
3. Search method 35

4. Possible sampling biases 36
5. Guaranteeing ethical standards 37
References 38
Ethics and social responsibility corporate strategy 39
Summary 40
1. Introduction 40
2. CSR theories and conceptual frameworks 41
3. Conclusion 44
References 45
General conclusion 48

MIX
Papier aus verantwortungsvollen Quellen
Paper from responsible sources
FSC® C105338

Printed by Books on Demand GmbH, Norderstedt / Germany